Walking in Total Freedom After Healing from Deep Inner Wounds

LaRose Angela Richardson

REJOICE
Essential Publishing

Copyright © 2019 by LaRose Angela Richardson

All rights reserved. No part of this publication may be reproduced by any means, graphics, electronic, or mechanical, including photocopying, recording, taping, or by any information storage retrieval system without the written permission of the publisher except in the case of brief quotations embodied in critical articles and reviews.

LaRose Angela Richardson/Rejoice Essential Publishing
PO BOX 512
Effingham, SC 29541

www.republishing.org

Unless otherwise indicated, scripture is taken from the King James Version.

"Scripture quotations taken from the Amplified® Bible (AMP), Copyright © 2015 by The Lockman Foundation Used by permission. www.Lockman.org"

Walking in Total Freedom After Healing from Deep Inner Wounds/ LaRose Angela Richardson

ISBN-10: 1-946756-68-7

ISBN-13: 978-1-946756-68-8

Library of Congress Control Number: 2019911969

"Walking in Total Freedom After Healing from Deep Inner Wounds," by LaRose Angela Richardson is a must-read. She is transparent and narrates her journey of heartache, betrayal, disappointments, and setbacks. The odds were stacked up against her, but she overcame. She could've stayed on the wrong path, but now she is on the straight and narrow. I admire her as a woman of wisdom and have learned a lot from her ministry. She is a woman of faith, and I witnessed God do the miraculous in her life. After reading this book, I gained a greater appreciation for her experiences. As you read the pages, you will attest to the fact that she is truly set free by the power of God. This book will encourage you to respond to challenges correctly and strengthen your relationship with the Lord.

Kimberly Moses, Author, Publisher, Magazine Editor of Rejoice Essential Magazine and Rejoice Essential Publishing

Table of Contents

ACKNOWLEDGMENTS..v

INTRODUCTION...1

CHAPTER 1:   Malice...............................7

CHAPTER 2:   Bitterness.......................11

CHAPTER 3:   Fear................................13

CHAPTER 4:   Generational
                  Curses...........................16

CHAPTER 5:   Self-Doubt....................27

CHAPTER 6:   Low Self-Esteem............33

CHAPTER 7:   Rejection......................36

CHAPTER 8:   Hopelessness.................39

CHAPTER 9:   Self-Hatred..................43

CHAPTER 10:	Abandonment..............47
CHAPTER 11:	Molestation...................51
CHAPTER 12:	Domestic Violence......................54
CHAPTER 13:	Grief...............................61
CHAPTER 14:	Betrayal.........................70
CHAPTER 15:	Insecurities...................74
CHAPTER 16:	Depression....................77
CHAPTER 17:	Salvation.......................82
CHAPTER 18:	Prayer............................85
CHAPTER 19:	Married for Purpose.........................89

ABOUT THE AUTHOR

Acknowledgments

I want to acknowledge my Lord and Savior, Jesus Christ, and the Holy Spirit for helping with the contents of the book. I like to thank the Holy Spirit for helping me overcome shame and embarrassment so I could tell my story and be a blessing to someone else. I pray they would be able to get free and walk in all that God has for them.

I like to acknowledge and thank Prophetess Kimberly Moses for challenging me and pulling me out of my comfort zone so that I can move forward in God.

I want to acknowledge my husband, Richard Richardson who is always encouraging me to continue to move forward. He is one of my biggest cheerleaders on the sidelines.

I like to acknowledge Prophetess Valora Cole for being obedient to God. She offered ten weeks of mentorship called "Fearless Intercessor." I received deliverance from the spirit of anger that was trying to destroy my life and destiny.

Introduction

Many people are wounded in their souls, emotions, and hearts when they were children. Much of which is not attributed to the children but to what is imposed upon them. Their parents and other family members, neighbors, and classmates may have contributed to the hurt that they endured. On some occasions, the unthinkable happened to these children, like incest, rape, molestation, abandonment, leaving a hole in their hearts and souls. Children should not be subjected to this type of trauma. We were taught to believe that adults are there to protect and not violate. Trauma has been something that many have kept silent about even up to adulthood.

It is possible wounding may have occurred when they were still in their mother's womb by things that were said or pronounced over the fetus by the mother or father of the child. It is said that babies can hear and feel things mothers go through while still in the womb. Some babies have even experienced botched abortions, which is when the mother thought that the baby was aborted but discovered later in the pregnancy that she was still pregnant with a live fetus. To the mother's amazement, her baby continued to live even after she tried to abort them. This type of trauma causes the child to feel unwanted by the parent. It also affects the child for the rest of their life. Their viewpoint of other relationships will suffer because of the unresolved hurt that they felt from what happened to them when they were a child. The only way hurt can be totally resolved is through deliverance because the child carries the spirit of rejection.

Another way rejection can occur is when a child is given up for adoption and the mother signs all parental rights away. The child goes to foster homes and sometimes orphanages but never feels like they belong to anybody. They feel as if nobody wants them to be part of their family, and they feel alone in this world.

Many children that are in the foster care system feel this way. However, other families have adopted many of them. As a result, they are made to feel like they belong to a family and have some meaning in life. While, I had a father in my life until I was 12 or 13 years old. I have never felt the love of a father until I gave my life to God, and then I felt the love that I have never experienced from my earthly father. I felt the unconditional love that only God can give.

According to Merriam-Webster, the definition of the soul is the moral and emotional nature of a human being.[1] This Scripture talks about soul and its prosperity, which is the greatest blessing on this side of heaven. 3 John 1:2 (Amp) says, "Beloved I pray that you may succeed and prosper and be in good health (physically), just as

(I know) your soul prospers (spiritually)." Grace and health are rich companions. Those that have prosperous souls will have healthy bodies. The Hebrew word for soul is "Nephesh" or Strong's # 5315.[2] The soul is the whole part of the person, the unity of the body, organs, and breath. It is your whole self or being.

When our souls are wounded and shattered, our whole being is infected with a type of virus. We can't function at full capacity because of the dysfunction. Just like a regular computer, when it has a virus, the CPU freezes up and must be fixed before it can function properly. Therefore, souls must be fixed with deliverance so that all the viruses can be eradicated from our core (heart) before moving further in life and in the things that God has for us.

In the book "God's Covenant with You for Deliverance & Freedom," by John Eckhardt, offers that deliverance is from God and part of the blessings of being in covenant with Him. It only destroys what is of the devil but never destroys what is of the Holy Spirit. Since deliverance is a work of the Holy Spirit, it builds up the saints and edifies the church. It tears down the strongholds of the enemy but builds up the work of God. Deliverance is the bread of the children of God. It is part of the spiritual diet from which every believer has a right to partake of it.[3]

In these scriptures, deliverance is referred to as the "Children's bread": In Mark 7: 26-28 (Amp) "Now the woman was a Gentile (Greek) a Syrophoenician by nationality. And she kept pleading with Him to drive the demon out of her daughter." "He was saying to her, "First let the children (of Israel) be fed, for it's not right to take the children's bread and throw it to the pet dogs (non-Jews)." But she replied, "Yes. Lord, but even the pet dogs under the table eat the children's crumbs."

There are several symptoms that can result from the soul rejected by parental figures. When rejection occurs in a child, it stays with them all through their adult life. As a result, every relationship that doesn't go in a positive way will continue to add fuel to the fire in their souls. After reading all this information, you will find the solution to the traumas, rejection, and soul wounds. You will learn how to find freedom in order to walk in wholeness through Christ Jesus.

CHAPTER 1

Malice

According to Merriam-Webster, the definition of a virus is something that poisons the mind or soul.[4] One of the most potentially poisonous substances is venom. Venom can be found in amphibians, animals such as snakes or spiders among other animals or marine life. If you are bitten or stung by a venomous creature, you must be sure to get some type of anti-venom or dire consequences may ensue.

Merriam-Webster defines venom as a spiteful malicious feeling or state of mind; extreme ill will.[5] Biblereason.com states that malice is the intention or desire to do evil.[5] It is the desire to inflict injury, harm, or suffering on someone else. Malice is a sin, and it's a big contributor to fighting and murder.[6] An example in the Scriptures of malicious murder was the killing of Abel by his brother Cain because of jealousy. Malice comes from the heart. Christians must avoid it by walking in the Spirit and putting on the whole armor of God.

Malice is something that is thought out and planned by a person to harm another person. Because they are upset with a person or an organization, someone will get on social media or some other platform to spread lies about a person. Malicious people don't have a conscious about what they are doing to a person or family because they are not happy about the good things that God is doing in their lives. Malicious people spread their malicious behavior to other people and infect them. They need a heart transplant so they can function in a better frame of mind.

Ezekiel 36:26 (Amp) says, "Moreover, I will give you a new heart and put a new spirit within you, and I will remove the heart of stone from your flesh and give you a heart of flesh." A heart of flesh can only come through knowing Jesus and making Him Lord of your life. God will give you a heart of flesh that is soft, tender, compassionate, and full of mercy complying with His Holy will. Renewing grace works as a change in the soul in turning a dead stone into living flesh. Only through Christ can we truly live again. We will take off the old man and put on the new man in Christ Jesus.

Ephesians 4:22-24 (Amp) says, "Strip yourselves of your former nature (put off and discard your old unrenewed self) which characterized your previous manner of life and becomes corrupt through lusts and desires that spring from delusions. "And be constantly renewed in the spirit of your mind (having a fresh mental and spiritual attitude). "And put on the new nature (the regenerate self) created in God's image (Godlike) in true righteousness and holiness."

According to perfectingofthesaints.com, the old man has rebelliousness, lust, worldliness, and pride in his DNA. These are called the "works of the flesh." The new man has the "fruit of the Spirit." In Galatians 5:19-23 you will find the nine fruits of the Spirit listed. Every believer is either walking in the flesh (yielded to the influence of the old man) or walking in the Spirit (yielded to the power of the new man). There is no middle ground.[7]

CHAPTER 2

Bitterness

Bitterness is caused by an expressive of severe pain, grief, or regret.[8] Act 8:23 (Amp) says, "For I see that you are provoked by bitterness and bound by sin." A person must practice forgiving, so that bitterness will not fester in their heart. Bitterness is a strong emotion, and if it is not dealt with, it can cause you to be stagnant in life making it very difficult to move forward. It is hard to forgive, but we must do it so that we can move on in life. Forgiveness is not for the other person, but it is for you. When we are living in offense, we tend to wear it like a piece of clothing by always bringing it up to people whenever the opportunity arises. According to a greatbiblestudy.

com article, it states that bitterness is a root. It is a source or a bubbling fountain that is laying under the surface. Most of the time, all it needs is some stressors to get the ball rolling. Bitterness is a deadly poison that needs to be brought into the light and addressed to bring many people out of spiritual, emotional, and even physical bondage.[9] When a person is bitter, it eats away at them like cancer. Many times, if we don't deal with the issue of bitterness, it starts attacking our health. Many types of cancer are due to the spirit of bitterness. Unforgiveness has festered in a person's heart, and they have not been delivered. If a person is delivered from these crippling emotions, they will receive healing in their bodies as well.

CHAPTER 3

Fear

Fear is to be in dread of someone or something as likely to be dangerous, painful, or threatening.[10] 2 Timothy 1:7 (Amp) says, "For God didn't give us the spirit of timidity or cowardice or fear, but (He has given us a spirit) of power and of love and of sound judgment and personal discipline (abilities that result in a calm, well-balanced mind and self-control). The spirit of fear is seen in many different forms. There are many types of phobias. A phobia is an extreme or irrational fear of or aversion to something. Most phobias can sometimes be related to traumatic incidents that happen in our lives.[12]

Nineteen million people in the United States have a phobia such as the following: .[11]

1. **Social phobia or social anxiety** - fear of the public and humiliation at being singled out or judged by others in a social situation.
2. **Agoraphobia** - fear of situations from which it would be difficult to escape. A person would experience extreme panic and freeze up in embarrassment.
3. **Claustrophobia** -fear of being in constricted confined spaces.
4. **Aerophobia** -fear of flying.
5. **Arachnophobia** - fear of spiders.
6. **Driving phobia** - fear of driving a car. This fear can be triggered after the person has recovered from an unfortunate accident.
7. **Emetophobia** -fear of vomiting.
8. **Erythrophobia** - fear of blushing.
9. **Hypochondria** -fear of becoming ill.
10. **Zoophobia** -fear of animals.

11. **Aquaphobia**- fear of water.
12. **Acrophobia** -fear of heights.
13. **Blood injury, and injection phobia** - fear of injuries, involving blood.
14. **Escalaphobia** -fear of escalators.
15. **Tunnel Phobia** -fear of tunnels.
16. **Illyngophobia** -the fear of vertigo.
17. **Ergophobia** -fear of work, manual labor, or performance anxiety.

All these phobias have a way of controlling our lives in the worst ways. Having been bought on by the lies of Satan, phobias are planted as seeds in your thought life. For this reason, it is so vital that the churches have deliverance ministries in operation. Jesus referred to deliverance as being very important for the children of God so they can function in the capacity that He intended. Each of us needs to operate in total wholeness, mind, body, soul, and spirit. Jesus has mercy on us and wants all of us fully delivered. You will read in the Bible many stories where Jesus had mercy on the sick and the ones who had demonic oppression. Jesus healed everyone that was brought to Him to be healed and set free.

CHAPTER 4

Generational Curses

Many curses and iniquities have come through family bloodlines. Many generational curses haven't been dealt with, so they have been passed down to third and fourth generation, as stated in Scripture. Deuteronomy 5:9 (Amp) says, "You shall not worship them or serve them; for I the Lord your God, am a jealous (impassioned) God (demanding what is rightfully and uniquely mine) visiting (avenging) the iniquity (sin, guilt) of the fathers, on the children (that is calling the children to account for the sins of their fathers), to the third and the fourth generations of those who hate me."

The enemy works to stay hidden through deception. He'll say that a Christian cannot have a demon, or that we have nothing that needs to be cast out. But that is a lie! Many Christians are demonically oppressed by many things that can be traced back to their great grandparents or that have trickled down through their bloodlines. Many things have been swept under the rug instead of dealing with the matter or casting out the issue. That is why things like cancer seem to be running rampant in certain families, because of undealt with issues. Just because we ignore or don't acknowledge something, doesn't mean that it is not there. Nor does it mean that it won't show up later down the generational lineage.

We must bind, cancel, and veto all generational curses to break them off the bloodline. It stops with you, and it will not go any further through the bloodline. You must come out of agreement with all sicknesses and diseases. These infirmities have no legal right to attack our bodies any longer.

My parents were on blood pressure medicine when they were living. Now my two brothers are on blood pressure medicine. Each of them takes more than one pill. I was also on blood pressure medicine from 2010 to 2013. By the grace of God one day, I was eventually able to get off them. Every time that I go to my doctor for a check-up, my blood pressure is textbook normal. It is 120/80 most of the time or somewhere within that range. I get so excited when they take my blood pressure and because I know that God truly healed me from that problem. I am no longer on any medication for my blood pressure. That generational curse is broken, and it stopped with me. I am healed by the blood of Jesus Christ. The greatest gift you can give your children is to break all the generational curses from off their lives. If the parents would take care of the iniquities and curses, then children and future generations can walk around healthy, whole and free from things in their bloodline.

John Eckhardt has a book called, "Prayers that Rout Demons," and several deliverance videos on YouTube as well.[13] He has another book called, "Fasting for Breakthroughs and deliverance."[14] He is known as the "general of deliverance" because he realizes the great need in the body of Christ for deliverance from different types of demonic oppression. Many people argue that Christians can't have a demon in them, but they can be demonically oppressed with various things like anger, fear, anxiety, panic attacks, bitterness, unforgiveness, and many other things. Many people are going to the doctor to be prescribed medications for issues when a deliverance service is truly needed. When churches start having deliverance services, people will get healed from demonic oppression. It will put a stop to all medicine doctors are prescribing.

Deliverance will put a stop to the pharmaceutical companies making millions of dollars on the shortcomings of their consumers. We need more deliverance ministries in this world today. We need someone that will go from city to city having deliverance services. Many children that are on medicine for 'Attention Deficit Disorder' would be able to come off their meds after they received deliverance from the oppression that is plaguing them. In the Bible, Jesus healed many people who were having seizures and this same deliverance power is available today.

Matthew 17:14-20 (Amp) says, "When they approached the crowd, a man came up to Jesus, kneeling before Him and saying, "Lord, have mercy on my son, for he is a lunatic (moonstruck) and suffers terribly; for he often falls into the fire and often into the water." "And I brought him to your disciples, and they were not able to heal him." "And Jesus answered, "You are unbelieving and perverted generation, how long shall I be with you? How long shall I put up with you? Bring him here to Me." "Jesus rebuked the demon, and it came out of him, and the boy was healed at once. Then the disciples came to Jesus privately and asked, "Why could we not drive it out?" "He answered, "Because of your little faith (your lack of trust and confidence in the power of God); for I assure you and most solemnly say to you, if you have (living) faith the size of a mustard seed, you will say to this mountain, "Move from here to there; and (if it is God's will) it will move; and nothing will be impossible for you."

We must pray and fast to get stubborn oppressions out of our bodies and lives. When we pray the Word of God back to Him, it obligates God to answer His word. Fasting means not eating or drinking for a period. It is done corporately or personally during certain days and times throughout the day. The definition of the word 'fast' is to abstain from food and eating sparingly or abstaining from some foods (Merriam Webster). Many fasts are available for you to try. The most popular one is the Daniel fast where you fast for 21 days only eating fruits and vegetables then drinking liquids.

Pray and ask God for different things that you may need in your life. Fasting also helps you receive the power to lay hands on the sick, and they shall recover. It helps to cast out demons and devils and to raise the dead. When we fast from food, we lay our agenda aside and pick up God's agenda on a situation. All Christians need to live a fasted lifestyle so we can walk in the authority that God has given us. When we turn our plate over to fast, pray and read the Word of God. Decree and declare it over a matter. What we are praying for will manifest in the natural realm after being released in the spiritual realm. We must fast with the right motives and not like the Pharisees and Sadducees. They fasted in a prideful manner to be seen, but we must fast with a spirit of humility.

Jesus went into the wilderness and fasted 40 days and 40 nights. He was tempted by the devil many times in Matthew 4: 1-7 (Amp), "Then Jesus was led by the (Holy) Spirit into the wilderness to be tempted by the devil. "After He had gone without food for forty days and forty nights, he became hungry. "And the tempter came and said to Him, "If You are the Son of God, command that these stones become bread." But Jesus replied, "It is written and forever remains written, "MAN SHALL NOT LIVE BY BREAD ALONE, BUT BY EVERY WORD THAT COMES OUT OF THE MOUTH OF GOD." Then the devil took Him into the holy city (Jerusalem) and placed Him on the pinnacle (highest point) of the temple. And he said (mockingly) to Him, "If You are the Son of God, throw Yourself down, for it is written, HE WILL COMMAND HIS ANGELS

CONCERNING YOU (TO SERVE, CARE FOR, PROTECT AND WATCH OVER YOU); AND THEY WILL LIFT YOU UP ON THEIR HAND, SO THAT YOU WILL NOT STRIKE YOUR FOOT AGAINST A STONE." Jesus said to him, "On the other hand, it is written and forever remains written, "YOU SHALL NOT TEST THE LORD YOUR GOD."

If you keep reading, you will see that every time the devil came to Jesus with a suggestion, Jesus cast it down with the Word of God. We should respond to the devil in this same manner. The more Word we know then, the more we cast the devil down when he tries to tempt us as well. The devil doesn't like us one bit. His job is to kill, steal, and destroy us, but Jesus came so that we can live abundantly in every area. Fasting brings us closer to God and helps get your body and flesh under control. When certain soulish desires try to magnify in your life, then the power of God through fasting and prayers gets rid of the issues and keeps them under control. Fasting means that you are radically handling the situation by taking away the things that your flesh likes and desires.

In Mark 9:29 (Amp) says, "He replied to them, "This kind (of unclean spirit) cannot come out by anything but prayer (to the Father)." Some things only go away with more effort and work like fasting and prayer. We want to give glory to God in all that we do for Him. If the word says that we need to fast, then that is what we should do so we can walk in the same power that raised Jesus from the dead. Jesus said in His word that we would do greater things than He did when He walked this earth. To get the same results that Jesus did, then we must do the same things that Jesus also did like fasting, prayer, and only saying what the Father told Him to say and do.

An article on Jentezenfranklin.org stated that the spiritual realm takes prayer and fasting to conquer things in the spirit. You will have petitions brought before God, which will not be answered during regular prayer, but if adding fasting with the prayer, then God will move heaven and earth to answer that prayer.[15] If we have family members, sons, daughters, husbands, or wives, who are out of the will of God or need healing, then we can start praying and fasting for them. Watch God change things around for your good and theirs.

I had a court case, which I needed to be decided in my favor. So, I called a prayer partner (someone I knew who was successful in prayer). We agreed to fast for three days, from 6 am to 6 pm. We drank nothing but liquids, mostly water each day. The fast started on a Wednesday and lasted to that Friday, which was the day I went to court. Friday morning, on my way to court, I called my prayer partner. We prayed, and I went to court with the confidence that God was going to move on my behalf. I went to court and testified. Afterward, I went home knowing that the victory was already won. A couple of months later, I received a letter in the mail stating that I had won my case. I knew that it was the prayer of agreement. Only God orchestrated the events that occurred that day. The court date was in April on Good Friday. The Judge and my lawyer's assistant both had medical backgrounds. I knew that God had already set the events in motion for it to come out in my favor.

We need to fast at least once a week or more as it will impact your experience in the Spirit. The method should be according to how you are led by the Holy Spirit. A person that doesn't fast is only reaping ½ of the benefits in their Christian walk. We will receive more power to walk in signs, wonders, and miracles in our ministries and churches, which is what is going to draw many people to Christ. When those people can see the demonstrations of the Spirit that the people of God are supposed to be moving in, their lives will change for the better by the redeeming power of Jesus Christ.

CHAPTER 5

Self-Doubt

According to Merriam-Webster, the definition of self-doubt is a lack of faith in oneself, a feeling of doubt or uncertainty about one's abilities, action, etc.[16]

Philippians 4:6-9 (Amp) says, "Do not be anxious for anything, but in everything (every circumstances and situation) by prayer and petition with thanksgiving, continue to make your (specific) request known to God." "And the peace of

God (that which reassures the heart, that peace) which transcends all understanding (that peace which) stands guard over your hearts and your minds in Christ Jesus (is yours)." "Finally, believers whatever is true, whatever is honorable, worthy of respect, whatever is right and confirmed by God's word, whatever is pure, and wholesome, whatever is lovely and brings peace, whatever is admirable and of good repute; if these is any excellence, if there is anything worthy of praise, think continually on these things (center your mind on them and implant them in your heart)." "The things which you have learned and received and heard and see in me, practice these things (in life daily) and the God (who is the source) of peace and well-being will be with you."

This scripture says to pray about everything and trust God to work all things out for your good. Meditate on God's Word planting it in heart. Think on the Word because God is the only one who can do something about your situation. Many Christians doubt their ability to do the things God has called them to do. When we look at God's grace instead of our ability, we can do anything but fail. God wants to use us for His

Glory, and He will equip us for the call that He has placed on our lives. God will give us the peace that passes all understanding in any situation in order to persevere through life here on earth. When praying, we are talking to God about our problems and listening to Him to speak to us concerning the solution to the problem we are facing in our lives.

We can either pray in English or tongues. When we pray in tongues, we are talking directly to God and are praying out of our spirits. We don't know what we are praying for, but our spirit does. Pastor Kenneth Copeland talks about "5 Benefits of Praying in Tongues" in an article on kcm.org,[17] This article states that when we are baptized in the Holy Spirit, we receive a gift from God which is the gift of speaking (or praying) in tongues. It is a powerful gift that every believer should desire.

5 BENEFITS OF SPEAKING IN TONGUES

1. Praying in Tongues allows you to speak directly to God. Neither you nor the people around you will be able to understand

what you are saying to God. You will be speaking by the power of the Holy Spirit inside of you (1 Corinthians 14:2).

2. Praying in Tongues keeps you in tune with the Holy Spirit. When praying in tongues, you are yielding to the Holy Spirit who dwells in you. Also, you are in tune with the Holy Spirit inside of you (Acts 2).

3. Praying in tongues strengthens your spirit. It builds you up spiritually and helps you to live a Spirit-led life (1 Corinthians 14:4).

4. Praying in tongues allows you to pray even when you don't know what to pray. Even when you don't know what to pray, you can still pray in tongues. You must trust your spirit to pray the perfect will of God. Romans 8:26

5. Praying in tongues is a weapon against the work of the enemy. Jesus proclaimed several things that would happen to those who followed Him and continued His work. Speaking allows Jesus' followers to stand against the wiles of the devil (Mark 16:15-18).

Sometimes we must be delivered from people's opinion about us. Other people's views do not matter as it does not validate or invalidate us. We are called by God to do a specific task in life. Honestly, no one is worthy on their own merits. We are not merited by the world's system but by God's system. He doesn't measure us by who we are currently but who we will be when He purifies us. God is in our future already. If we could see ourselves the way God sees us, then we would be better in this life. Man looks at the outer appearance, but God looks at the heart of the matter. He looks at our hearts and knows that we are capable of being and doing what He has called us to be and do by grace. We must remember that people will scrutinize us if we do good or bad. However, our aim must always be to do good, so we can stay under the umbrella of God grace. It is not your responsibility to prove or conform yourself for anyone's pleasure. Our goal in this life should be to please God and Him alone.

Galatians 1:10 (Amp) states, "Am I now trying to win the favor and approval of men, or of God? Or am I seeking to please someone? If I were still trying to be popular with men, I would not be a bondservant of Christ!" When you are pleasing God, man will not always agree with you. Depend on God and Him only, not man. Give your all to Christ, and He will take care of your needs. We are not to try to please men to the point that we are sinning, which leads us out of the will of God. I would rather be in God's will any day and have a close relationship with Him than to be a man-pleaser. Man is a fickle being. People will like you today, and then tomorrow they are unreasonably mad at you. If God is pleased with you, then you are operating in the will of God for your life. Stay in the will and keep moving forward in the things of God for your life.

CHAPTER 6

Low Self Esteem

Low self-esteem is characterized by a lack of confidence and feeling badly about oneself.[18] People with low self-esteem often feel unlovable or incompetent. Satan wants us to stay in captivated by low self-esteem because he knows that if we truly find our place and start operating in the will of God, we will be a major threat to him because we would lead many people to Christ. Most of the time, this emotion is due to something that happened in a person's childhood that made them feel inadequate about something in their lives. Maybe they were bullied in school about the way they looked or dressed, which made them feel less of a person. Many times, when these issues are not dealt with in adolescent years, individuals tend to get into abusive relationships either verbally, mentally, or physically.

Some may ask themselves, "Why does this keep happening to me? Why do I keep picking abusive people to be in a relationship with? What is wrong with me? I can't do anything right!" Most of the time, they are their own biggest critics, which is a dysfunction that can be broken with deliverance and renewing their mind with the Word of God daily. They must speak it out loud what God says about because the Word says, "that faith comes by hearing, hearing the word of God." We must speak it out loud to get it in our spirit. We must take the Word of God as if it was your regular prescribed medication. Whether it be twice a day, three times a day, or even four times a day, you decide according to your need to confess these declarations. There are many more in the Bible, but here are a few to help you get started.

Say these out loud.

I am fearfully and wonderfully made (Psalm 139:14).
I am above and not beneath (Deuteronomy 28:13).
I am the righteousness of God (2 Corinthians 5:21).
I am loved by God (Psalm 136:26, Zephaniah 3:17, John 3:16).
God knows my name and it is written on His hand (Isaiah 49:16).
I can do all things through Christ who strengthens me (Romans 8:28).
He knew me before I was formed in my mother's wound (John 10:14-15).

When we realize how much God loves us and cares about us, we would not worry about anything because He wants the best for all of us. We need to depend on Him for all the things that we will need in life. Matthew 6:33 (Amp), "But first and most important seek (aim at, strive after) His kingdom and His righteousness (His way of doing and being right- the attitude and character of God), and all these things will be given to you."

CHAPTER 7

Rejection

According to Merriam-Webster, the definition of rejection is the action of rejecting a state of being rejected (refuse) to accept, consider, submit to.[19] In Psalm 34:17-20 (ESV), "When the righteous cry for help, the Lord hears and delivers them out of all their troubles." The Lord is near to the brokenhearted and saves the crushed in spirit." "Many are the afflictions of the righteous, but the Lord delivers him out of them all. He keeps all his bones; not one of them is broken."

We are rejected by an assortment of people during our lifetime here on earth. But in Isaiah 53, we see how Jesus was despised and rejected by his own people, the Jews. They wouldn't receive Him as the Messiah that was prophesied in Scripture. To this day, many of them are still looking for the Messiah.

The Word states that if we are God's children, then we will also be rejected. Just know that we are never alone. Jesus said, "That He would never leave or forsake us, but would be with us until the end of the world." Jesus understands how it feels to be rejected, beaten, spat upon, and lied on. So, we can rest assured that whatever we go through for the sake of Christ, He knows about it. When people reject what we are doing for Christ, if we are in His will, they are not just rejecting you, but the Jesus that is in you. To this day, people are still rejecting Jesus when they refuse to give their lives to Him and live a life that is pleasing to Him.

God gave everyone a free will. He will not force anyone to serve Him or live for Him. It is your choice to surrender your life totally to him and proclaim that Jesus is truly Lord over your life.

Getting over rejection is a process, but it can be done with the help of the Lord. If we are living in this world, we are all subject to be rejected at some point in our lives. But with the love of God living in us when we are rejected, we will continue to show love regardless of the situations. Rejection will become a thing of the past in our lives and will not stop us from moving forward in life.

CHAPTER 8

Hopelessness

According to Merriam-Webster, hopelessness is having no expectation of good or success, despairing incapable of improvement.[20]

Revelation 21:4 (Amp) says, "He shall wipe all tears from their eyes. "There will be no more death, no more grief, no more crying or pain." "The old things have disappeared."

Hopelessness is a crippling thing. When you are going through something that seems so hard, you can't see any relief in the situation. The more you try to get out of the slump, the worst it gets sometimes. When a marriage breaks up, and everyone goes their separate ways, you begin to feel a sense of hopelessness. You want the pain to stop in order to be healed.

In Mark 5:25-26, the woman with the issue of blood felt like she was in a hopeless situation. She had been bleeding for twelve long years non-stop. Perhaps she was weak in her body since her hemoglobin was low. Maybe she felt drained and didn't even feel like going to meet Jesus, but she knew that she had to push her way through so she could get her healing. She went from doctor to doctor and spent all her money trying to find a cure for her bleeding disorder. She probably tried all types of treatments, but none of them worked for her. But when she heard that Jesus was passing by, so she made up her mind that if I don't get to Jesus today, I may not see another year. She saw Jesus in the crowd, so she pushed her way through the crowd. She fell to her knees, crawled, and grabbed the hem of his garment.

Jesus felt the virtue when it left him and entered her body. He knew someone had just received their healing. Her faith was so strong and relentless that she knew within herself that when she touched his garment, she would receive everything that she needed that day to be made whole.

Jesus immediately felt when the virtue left him. He asked, "Who touched me?" Then the disciples asked, "What you do mean who touched you?" The crowd was so massive that everyone was bumping into one another. But this touch was different from just bumping into someone. Her faith had pulled on Jesus and healing manifested in her body that day. Perhaps she left there hopeful for a future and knowing that Jesus is a healer. He had met her need that day. It doesn't say this in the Scripture, but maybe everyone that she met she told them of the miracle she received when she touched Jesus garment that day. If we would have the same faith and hope in Jesus as she did that day, Jesus would do the same for us regardless of what we need him to do. She knew that by the Law, she wasn't even supposed to be in a public place.

Her singular focus was: "I got to get to Jesus!" "I got to get to Jesus!" Her body was healed from that one touch. She received a supernatural blood transfusion from Jesus that glorious day. Jesus wants to heal us of all from our sicknesses and illnesses. He wants every one of us well. Will you accept your healing? Be healed and set free from all your infirmities in Jesus' name. Amen. Do you have faith the size of a mustard seed to receive your healing today? When we worship, fast, and pray, it brings changes in our lives for the better. Then we enter the holy place in the presence of God.

CHAPTER 9

Self-Hatred

Self-hatred is disdain of oneself rather than others (Merriam Webster).[21] Ephesians 5:29 (ESV) says, "For no one ever hated his own flesh, but nourishes and cherishes it, just as Christ does the church." Paul continues his focus on husbands loving their wives. Paul explains that husbands are to love their wives as themselves. A man nourishes and cares for his body. In the book, "40 Day Fast," Rebecca King offers that self-hatred hides well. Self-hatred throws fiery flames of blame and shame while bombarding one's mind with hopelessness that desires to destroy the depth of one's destiny. Blame originates with shame, and then shame causes bitterness. Self-hatred tells your mind that you are the enemy, and then the mind attacks the body. Self-hatred sabotages all success and usually offers one explanation of excuses that will hinder any progress of encouragement. Self-hatred raises the body's stress levels and weakens the immune system. Self-hatred is what the enemy uses when he cannot find anything else to destroy us.[22]

Forgive yourself for not loving yourself and be set free. Self-hatred is predominant in the entertainment industry. While watching television, the average teenage girl sees models that are slim and trim with flat abs. This could initiate in them body image issues where they question their own weight and size. They could begin to starve themselves, eat, and then throw up. These disorders have had many teenage girls close to death at times. They may be skin and bones, but all they can see, and think is that they are fat instead of loving the body God gave them. They aren't content with the way that He made them.

I remember in my childhood where I was skinny and tall. When I used to wear shorts in the summertime, I would sometimes get negative comments from other girls about how skinny my legs were. There was a guy with them one day. He told them that my legs were the right size for my body. I only weighed 95 pounds and wore XS in clothing. I wore this size up to my adult years until I was in my 30s. I only started gaining weight after I had a total hysterectomy when I was 42 years.

I am at a comfortable weight now. My clothes fit my body just right. My dad's side of the family is obese. I had an aunt who died of complications from being morbidly obese. I took after my mom's side of the family where everyone is slender, built, and a healthier size. I love to eat and never had any issues with obesity. I love to cook and try new recipes to critique them to fit my taste.

When we don't love ourselves, we believe Satan's lie, that we are not good enough. This lie is not the truth because we are made in the image of God. We are masterpieces, and God didn't make any mess or junk when He created us. Remember that God loves us no matter our size, shape, color, or nationality. He loves us all the same regardless of what we don't have. All of us have abilities, talents, and gifts, which are unique and differ from others. You have something you do best. Never compare yourself to anyone else because we are all important to God. He will use us to accomplish the calling He has placed on our lives. We are all unique and special in our own way.

CHAPTER 10

Abandonment

I experienced abandonment when I was 12 or 13 years old. My dad left our family. He left my mom, two brothers and I. We didn't know where he was or how to find him. He walked away from the responsibility of taking care of his family to move in with another woman without children. He had already left us in a sense because every Friday when he would get paid, he would get dropped off at the local hole in the wall in my town. By the time he made it home, he was sloppy drunk and broke. I remember plenty of days that he would come back cussing, fussing, and reeking of alcohol. He would get so drunk that he would urinate all over the chair that he was sitting in. The chair had to be thrown away. My mom wasn't working at the time when he left, and all the bills were at the final notice stage.

Thank God for my grandmother, who lived two houses down from us. She was working by cleaning other people's homes at that time. She was able to help my mom keep the utilities on until my mom could find a job. My mom got a job at one of the local motels cleaning rooms. She eventually got us food stamps so we could have food to eat. I remember when I was getting ready to graduate from High School. I reached out to my father and told him the good news. I invited him to graduation. He found every excuse not to attend my graduation, and he didn't show. Also, he didn't come to my second graduation from Southeastern Technical Institute for Practical Nursing in 1997.

My mom got sick in 2008 and passed away in April of that year. I informed my father about the arrangements. He wouldn't come to my mom's funeral to support my two brothers and I during our grief. At this point, I began to wonder, what was the problem? I went to him after the funeral to see why he didn't come. He said that he had forgotten about the funeral, but I guess that excuse was better than no excuse No matter what I tried to do, I could not make him love me like a father should love a child. So, I just gave up trying at that point.

I thank God that I was able to forgive and move on with my life. In 2000, he was diagnosed with stage 4 lung cancer. He refused to do any radiation or chemotherapy. He lived up until December 2015. Before he died, God allowed me to lead him to Christ. I know that I went through all of this for a purpose. It has made me stronger and able to handle situations I thought I wouldn't be able to handle. I have a Heavenly Father, Abba Father, who has been the father that I have never experienced on this earth. Father God is always with me. He never leaves me. He has been my mother and father at the same time. I can go to Him and talk about anything that may come up in my life. I have no need of anyone but God to validate my relationship as His daughter. No longer do I have to feel as if I am alone in this world. Daddy God is with me.

CHAPTER 11

Molestation

I remember being molested as a young girl. I thought that since it was being done to me, I didn't have a choice in the matter and that no one cared. I didn't know any better. Even after it was found out and brought to the light, nothing was done about it. I was still allowed to be around the person who was doing it. That is why I took the path that I chose in life.

I got married when I was young at 19 years old then moved away to another city with my husband. That was one of the worst mistakes that I made in my youth because the guy that I married was an undercover alcoholic. When he and his sisters would come to our house, they all would get sloppy drunk. That was the first time I saw a woman get sloppy drunk where she didn't know where she was. Not a pretty sight.

I remember one day they had been drinking. They wanted to get something to eat. Since I didn't drink, and I took them to a restaurant in the city we were living in. All three of them showed out so bad that I took my food, got up, and went to sit in the car until they had eaten, then I drove home. They were so embarrassing. They cussed and talked loud enough for everyone in the restaurant to hear them. You can't take some people anywhere. I learned my lesson that day. If they weren't sober, then I wasn't going anywhere with them hungry or not. I wasn't a drinker because I saw how alcohol made them act.

I certainly didn't want any part of the scene, not to mention my dad was an alcoholic. I stayed in that marriage so long to the extent that I wanted to do some bodily harm to him. I knew it was time to leave and never come back. I packed up my stuff on Monday because on Mondays he traveled out of town to work. He was a brick mason, and he would come back on Fridays. On this Monday, he left, but he came back home. I already had my stuff packed and had already gone to my job to tell them that I was quitting. When he came home, we had an altercation. He threw me down on the floor and started choking me. I made clear that I was and moving back home. He told me that he would kill me. I told him that I was leaving the house one on my own or in a body bag.

At that point in my thinking, I wanted to do some bodily harm to him. The best thing for me to do was to leave. I knew if he came home drunk again and started messing with me, then something bad would probably happen. So, to avoid that, the best thing to do was leave. He let me go, and I haven't looked back. I moved in with my grandmother and stayed there until I moved into my apartment.

CHAPTER 12

Domestic Violence

Then after living in my hometown for a year, I met another man whom I thought was a good man until I married him. I found out he had serious issues with being crazy jealous. We would be riding down the road and I would look out the window. If a man was in a yard along the road, he would say, "What are you looking at? Let's go back and see what you found so interesting in the yard?" It got so bad that I always rode in the car with him driving with my head down. I never looked anyone in the eyes because he was always trying to say I wanted to be with someone else. I had no interest in anyone else but him. But after a year, I didn't even want to deal with him any longer.

I asked God, "What is the problem with all these crazy men that I keep getting hooked up with?" I was married to him for two years, but I had taken all that I could from this man. Everything seemed like it started going south when I finished nursing school and got my Nursing License. I got a job making more money than him. I also got a new car. He started being more abusive after that.

I had so much stress that my hair started falling out. I didn't realize it until I went to the beauty shop one day. The beautician asked me what was going on. My husband at the time got a job as a housekeeper at the local nursing home where I was working. He made my life a living hell. I was always confronted about something or someone that I had to work with at the nursing home. He was lurking around every corner it seemed. He couldn't have been doing his work because trying to watch me so much.

I was going to church a few miles from where we were living at the time. I had to go a few extra miles to pick up my mom and brothers so we could go to church together. When we attended revival meetings at night, I would have to take my mother and brothers home very late, which would make my arrival home after 11 pm. My husband went to ranting and raving. He said that I needed to be home and in the house by 11 pm. This was completely unrealistic because I worked the 3-11 shift at the nursing home. Now simply because I wanted to go to the revival, I suddenly needed to be home now before 11 pm?

This man certainly had split personalities. He started staying out all night and called me to tell me that it was my fault that he wasn't coming home that night. I told him that I wasn't happy anymore and was leaving him. I found a home next door to my mom. He left to go to work one morning and I packed my stuff so that I could leave the home without a confrontation. It didn't happen as I had planned. He came back from work and found me packing to leave. He told me if I left that I wouldn't be able to get back in the house and get the rest of my belongings. He took the house key from me. I left with my car packed down with everything that I could bring with me. He called me later and told me that he left the rest of my stuff on the carport. So, I rented a U-Haul and got the rest of my belonging from the carport. The strange thing about this whole matter is I left him the day after our anniversary. There was nothing happy about that anniversary.

I ended up dating someone a couple of years later that was abusive too. So, I just quit trying after that. I realize that if you don't get healed of the wounds in your heart and soul, then you will end up with the similar destructive experience. I swore off men at that point and refused to date anyone. If I engaged in any relationships with men, they could only be platonic. Nothing they did would impress me. I dated off and on through the next couple of years. I always seemed to attract the same kind of man. It was a different person, but it still ended in some abusive behavior. The last person I dated before I refused to date anyone else, I had to end up putting a restraining order on him to get him to stop harassing me after I broke up with him. I refused to compromise any longer. I met him at the club, so I quit going to clubs and started staying home. I refused to date and remained celibate for several years. I believed that I had heard every line (lie) by then anyway. From then on, no matter who asked me to go out on a date or out to eat, the answer was no. Many tried to set me up on blind dates. The answer was still no.

By this time, I had truly surrendered to Christ and was celibate. I got more into the church that I was going to at the time. I swore off men until God would send me the right one. Jesus was enough for me at that point. People tried to set me up with dates, but I refused to compromise any longer. I was tired of being misused and abused by men. I love myself, and I don't have to settle for less to know that I am important. I receive my validation from God and Him only.

"I am free! Praise the Lord! I am free! I am no longer bound! No more chains are holding me!" This was the song that I sang after leaving that marriage. A month later, I received a phone call from one of the local lawyers in my town to sign the divorce papers. I didn't hesitate because I wanted out of that marriage.

Then I heard a wedding announcement on the radio. My ex-husband was getting married, yet again, to someone that didn't know any better. A month after that, he sent me a letter stating that he had made a mistake when he married the other woman. He wanted us to get back together. He stated that we could move to another place and start over. I wondered: "What is wrong with this man?" Then I showed the letter to my mom. She shook her head in disbelief. I told him, "No. I don't want to be in a relationship with you any longer. I wish you all the best in your new marriage. I have had enough of your verbal abuse, emotional abuse, and physical abuse. Enough is enough! Stay married and leave me alone."

I've never looked back since then. God answered my prayer and delivered me when I asked Him. I wasn't going back into that confusion because I was already free from it. Do not stay in an abusive relationship because you deserve much more than that. God wants us to have the very best in every area of our lives. No more settling when I am a daughter of the Most High God. I know that He wants me to have the best of everything.

CHAPTER 13

Grief

In December 2007, my mom started getting sick. She was having trouble breathing and felt like she couldn't catch her breath most of the time. Then she started losing weight. I took her to her doctor's appointment about 45 minutes from where we lived. The doctor wrote an order for her to have an X-ray of her lungs to discover the reason for the difficulty in breathing. I took her to the hospital to have her X-rays. When they put her on the table to do the X-ray, they found that her lungs were black. Only about half of the right lung was working resulting in the feeling of not being able to couldn't catch her breath.

I was really upset with the findings and would go home every night to pray for her. We went back to her next appointment for the doctor to read the X-rays and tell her what they saw on them. The doctor informed her that she had lung cancer and that she would be sending her to a hospital that was an hour away from where we lived. I asked to take off from my job so that I could take her to her appointment. When we went there, the doctor informed my mom that there was nothing they could do. If they could have caught it before this last stage, they probably could have given her Chemotherapy. I found out later that she already knew about her diagnosis, but she just kept it to herself until she couldn't withhold it anymore.

I was devastated because I knew that it would be a matter of days before she would be leaving me. I cried all the time and prayed. I told my family that she didn't have much longer to be here and they didn't believe me. I had seen the outcome in a dream one night, and I knew. I felt that

God was showing me so I could get everything prepared for her.

It got to the point that she had lost so much weight she was unable to take care of herself. She had stopped eating. The smell of food made her sick on the stomach, and she couldn't eat. I would bathe her and dress her for bed. Before I would go home every day on my way to work, I would stop by to check on her. I would get her up and dress her. I'd even got off work one day and found that she had fallen in the bathroom when she tried to get off the toilet. She was okay. Nothing was broken by the grace of God. I stayed at her house late. I bathed and dressed her for bed.

I went home that night and dreamed that she would be leaving sooner than I thought. It was a Friday. I remember because we were going to get paid that day. I remember telling my supervisor about the dream and asking her if I could leave so I could take my mom to the emergency room. After I got through giving out my noon medication to my patients, I called my uncle. I told him about my mother, and he agreed to meet us at the hospital. I had to borrow a wheelchair from my mother's neighbor because she was so weak, she could not walk. Upon arriving at the Emergency Room, we immediately went to the triage and were assigned a room. The nurses tried to start an IV but it five sticks before they were successful. I stayed with her all night. We talked, and I asked her, "What did she want to do? Do you want to be on life support?" She said, "No."

I didn't sleep much because I knew what was coming. So, I got up the next morning to go home to bathe and change clothes, and then I would return to the hospital. As soon as I stepped inside my home, I got a call from the hospital telling me that my mom had taken a turn for the worst and that she would be moving to ICU. The nurse stated that she had asked my mom if she wanted life support. My mom told her no. I wanted the nurse to honor my mother's wishes.

I jumped in the shower, put my clothes on and packed a bag so I could stay in town. I called my stepdad, my brothers, aunts, uncles, cousins, our pastor, and church family to let them know what was going on. I picked up my brother and stepdad then we headed to the hospital. As we entered the

ICU, the nurses told us to wait just a few minutes until they could get her comfortable. The doctor came out and told us that the fluids that they had given her had gone into her lungs, resulting in pneumonia. He also said that there wasn't anything else they could do but make her comfortable. I had to hold it together for my brothers and stepdad, so I went into her room. Mom was already aware of the pneumonia and resting comfortably.

I left the room to call everyone ensuring they knew she would be leaving this worldly very shortly due to pneumonia. Everyone I called came and sat with us that entire day. She made her peace with God and everyone that went into that room. I felt like she was trying to hold on for me. So, I went into her room and told her, "Momma, you don't have to try to hold on for me. I will be taken care of. I am closer to God than you think."

When visiting hours were over at the hospital, I tried to stay, but they wouldn't let me. So, I went to stay with a friend in town. I got in the shower to take a bath. When I finished, there was a call from the hospital. They stated, "That we needed to come in a hurry." I called everyone that was there that day, and they came back to meet us at the hospital. We prayed and sang songs. My mom took her cover off and tried to get up. I put the cover back on her. Next, she decided to take her oxygen mask off, but I put it back on. Then I told her if she wanted to take it off that she could. She took it off, took two breaths, and left this world. We all cried, but I had to pull it together because I had to take care of her business. I had to be strong for everyone else.

After I composed myself, I came out of the room to make a couple of calls. I called the funeral home. As I was talking to the nurse, she told me, "It is rare that we have two people to die at the same time." Someone had died across the hall, so I went and looked in the room. I saw the Director of Nursing from my job crying in the room. I went in and consoled her family. I told them that, "They are in heaven. In heaven there it is no more suffering or pain. They are free from pain."

After the funeral home came to pick her up, I went to her house. I tried to go to sleep, but

I couldn't. I cried all night because her death crushed me. I had an appointment to meet the funeral director the next day. So, I went next door to tell my Aunt, and she was acting strange. I went back to my mom's house to start cleaning up for company. My Uncle came, and I told him to check on my Aunt. He came back and stated that he had to get her up off the floor. I went back over to her house and tried to talk to her. She wasn't responding, so I sent her to the ER with other family members while I met with the funeral director.

I received a call from the ER nurse, asking me questions about my Aunt. So, I left and went to the hospital. They told me that she had a stroke. I informed them of my mother's death the previous night. I asked them if they would call her doctor and put her in a room because I knew that it would only be a matter of time for her as well. I went home that night and took something in order to sleep. I got a call for me to come to the hospital quickly. I asked for them to contact my Uncle because I know that I couldn't deal with death two nights in a row. I got up the next day and went to my mom's house. I found out my

Aunt passed away only a couple of hours after the hospital had called. When my mom passed, it seemed like a dream. When my Aunt passed the next day, it all became a reality.

We were all blown away. Instead of preparing for one funeral, now I was preparing for two. By the grace of God and prayer, I received a double dose of strength to make it through this trial. I know other people were praying for me, as well. At the funeral, the spirit of God was strong, and I had to dance it out. I kissed them both goodbye and said, "I will see you both again in Heaven."

I finally went back to work. Mother's Day and my mom's birthday were both coming up, so I requested off. I stayed home and prayed. I asked God for more strength. I told Him, "Lord if you don't help me, I am not going to make it." He gave me more strength to carry on, which is why I can write about it now. I do get a little teary-eyed when I tell the story because it brings back memories of a difficult time in my life. When it was fresh on my mind, I would read John 14:1-14 every day before I would go to work. Sometimes at night, if I thought about it the grief, God's word has helped me get through it. I laid on my face before the Lord while crying out to Him many times throughout the years. I prayed, not when things were going wrong, but all the time because a time may come that I can't pray. I will have prayers stored up already, and God can use them.

CHAPTER 14

Betrayal

During the time of losing my mother and aunt, my stepdad was acting up badly. He kept making statements around me and other family members such as, "I am glad God took them out of their misery." All I could do was to hold my peace. He was bringing women around to the house that he was already messing with before my mom died. He showed no respect for her, me, and the rest of the family. I had to pray hard for God to give me the strength to get through the craziness. I was cleaning out my mom's room, and he wanted me to get all her stuff out of his house by a certain deadline. He wanted her things moved to my home or my brother's house. My stepdad showed no remorse, real love, or grief during the passing of my mother or my aunt.

The week after the funeral, he had moved another woman into the house quickly, which was very disrespectful. I would go home and lay before the Lord every night. I asked God to help me keep from getting in the flesh and physically harming him for the way that he was disrespecting my mother. We hadn't even buried her or prepared all the funeral arrangements yet. He was acting like a snake. When I told my cousins what he was doing and the things that he was saying, they wanted to get physical with him. I told them, "No. We will let God deal with him about his behavior." God was truly on my side through this trying time of my life. He kept me from acting out of character and gave me the strength to hold my peace so that he could fight my battles for me.

On a Saturday morning in May, we had a double funeral since it was all the same family attending both funerals. My Pastor preached the funeral. Also, we let my Aunt's Pastor say a few words about my Aunt and Mother. My mom's nieces and nephew sang the songs that were our favorites. I felt that day that I had done all that I could for them while they were on this earth and a peace came over me at this time. I dreamed about the funeral several months before when my mom first got sick. Everything that I saw in the dream was being shown now at both of their funerals. I believe the Lord was preparing me for the events to come ahead of time.

After much study, I discovered years later that He possibly wanted me to intercede for them in order to change the outcome of the dream. Now I thank God for the growth that has happened in my life as it pertains to understanding the meaning of dreams. Now I know through study and prayer what God called me to do is intercession. I need to fortify people by praying for them. God will change the outcome in their lives through prayer. The fervent prayer of the righteous availeth much. I am to pray until I see heaven rain down the answer. Giving up prayer for a person is not an option because I know that prayer works.

It will continue to work if I keep my hand in Jesus' hands and be obedient to His word.

CHAPTER 15

Insecurities

According to Merriam-Webster, insecurities are not the feeling of being unconfident or sure, deficient in assurance, beset by fear and anxiety.[23]

Ephesians 6:10-11,13-17 (AMP) says, "In conclusion, be strong in the Lord (be empowered through your union with Him); draw your strength from Him (that strength which His boundless might provide)." "Put on the whole armor (the armor of heavy-armed soldier which God supplies), that you may be able to successfully stand up against (all) the strategies and the deceits of the devil." "Therefore, put on God's complete armor, that you may be able to resist and stand your ground on the evil day (of danger), and having done all (the crisis demands), to stand (firmly in your place). "Stand therefore (hold your ground), having tightened the belt of truth around your loins and having put on the breastplate of integrity and of moral rectitude and right standing with God." "And having shod your feet in preparation (to face the enemy with the firm-footed stability, the promptness, and the readiness produced by the good news) of the Gospel of peace." "Lift up over all the (covering) shield of saving faith, upon which you can quench all the flaming missiles of the wicked (one)." "And take the helmet of salvation and the sword that the Spirit wields, which is the Word of God."

I have times of insecurity because of the many things that I have endured over my life. I tend to get so nervous and anxious when I am around certain people because I felt like I don't measure up to them. God has taught me that it doesn't matter what other people think about my qualifications in ministry. God's opinion is the only one that matters. Even if other people don't agree with the calling that God has on my life, it doesn't matter. God will equip me for the tasks that He has set before me. I know that God is with me, and He hears my prayers. He is very concerned about my well-being. God has rescued me my entire life from things I willingly walked into and traps the devil has set up for me.

In "Overcoming Insecurity in a Woman's Life by Robin Weidner" she states: "Stop wasting time and energy looking for security from your money, your health, your husband or boyfriend, your friends, your job, your beauty or anyone or anything else that is not God Himself. God is the only true source of security. Security can only be found in the peace God offers you through Jesus. Embrace your identity as God's beloved child and be assured that through your relationship with Jesus, you will have all the power you need to do God's will in every situation."[24]

CHAPTER 16

Depression

Estimates reveal that 20% of adults will experience at least one bout of serious clinical depression in their lifetime (ask-angels.com). Many are facing a lifelong struggle with depression. Depression is more than just a miserable day here and there. It is more than disappointments because you don't get the job, the guy, or a dream house. Someone suffering from depression faces a daily battle against hopelessness.[25] Depression is when you seem to lose all sense of joy derived from things you used to enjoy doing. Now they have become meaningless to you.

When I was going through a bout of depression, I was having trouble sleeping because my mind was always trying to figure something out. I stayed awake for days at a time until finally, I had to go to the doctor to get something to help me sleep. My body was fatigued, and my blood pressure was elevated. I had to start taking blood pressure medication. Albert Einstein quoted, "We can't solve problems by using the same kind of thinking we used when we created them.[26] We have to realize that we have to change our perspective about a matter. If we are thinking negative, then negative things will usually manifest. We must start thinking positively and meditate not on what we see in the natural but what can't see in the spiritual realm.

I remember being depressed about certain things when I was younger. I would cry sometimes. As an adult, I was stressed out about life, especially grieving over the death of my mom and domestic violence situations I had experienced. Even after I got married in 2009, it was hard for me to find a job down in the area where I lived, losing a home, and my husband being out of a job as weather kept preventing his ability to work; all were very stressful for me.

I ended up going back to work at the nursing home where I was previously employed. I had to drive a whole hour to get to work. I was working 7 am-3 pm shifts and had to be up around 4 am in order to make it to work by 6 am, which was very stressful. The nursing home cut down on help, and it left all the nurses stressed out because of a double the workload without adequate pay.

I remember one day after I got off from work, my back was hurting me terribly. So, I went to the doctor to get it checked. I ended up having to get an MRI because of the pain, and they found a slipped disc. I had to quit my job because I was in so much pain. I knew that being a charge nurse and working the floor was a thing of the past for me. I had several epidurals that didn't relieve the pain, so I had back surgery in May 2015, on my L4, L5, S1 vertebrae with a spinal infusion. It took eight weeks for me to recover.

I initially felt better until December 2015. When I started having numbness in my right leg, I went back to the doctor. They did another MRI and found that the hardware had slipped. I needed surgery again to repair the damage. In April 2016, I proceeded to have surgery again but this time to fix the problem. I did well after that. In January of 2018, I started to have nerve pain in my left leg. I went back to the doctor where they ordered a CT of the left leg. They found that bone spurs were lying on my sciatic nerve in my left lower buttock area. My whole left leg was numb. In March 2018, I went in for my last surgery to shave the bone so it would stop pressing against my sciatic nerve. I had a quick recovery, which was a blessing. In January 2019, I started going to the Fitness Center to do light workouts on the stationary bike and treadmill.

My health is optimal right now. I am receiving spiritual healing through being a part of a prayer line every day at 6 am and 12 pm from Monday through Friday. It has empowered me to be better spiritually and to pray with power over a situation. We have a sisterhood on the prayer line too. I am no longer depressed. God has delivered me from that oppression. Now I know how to speak the Word to depression if it rises again in my life.

CHAPTER 17

Salvation

Salvation is one of the most important things that we can do in our lives. It not only determines where you will spend eternity, but it is a security blanket. When you surrender your life to Jesus, it brings about a change in your life. When I gave my life to Christ, it was the best decision I have ever made because I was so deep in sin. I just got tired of going around the same mountain year after year and never progressing in life. I would pray to God and ask Him to help me. I was sick and tired of being sick and tired. I knew there had to be something better in life than what I was experiencing.

One Friday Night at my church, there was a revival with a visiting Evangelist from Louisiana. After he preached a sermon, he conducted an altar call. I went up to the altar and accepted Christ as the head of my life. The revival lasted about two months. I was asked to lead praise and worship. I remember during that time, there were many miracles, signs, and wonders happening. The Shekinah Glory would show up and wreck the place. This was my first experience of being around the Glory of God so strong like that. The Glory of God would show up when I went to church growing up, but nothing compares to the strength I experienced that night.

I have always loved to read, so I would purchase books. I studied about being saved and the Holy Spirit. Now there are webinars that help you learn what it takes to become the man or woman of God that God wants you to be by the power of the Holy Spirit. I have signed up for webinars on the Prophetic, Prophetic Activations, Mentorships of the Fearless Prayer Warrior,27 a teaching prayer line, all of which has kept me empowered and encouraged to keep going on.

CHAPTER 18

Prayer

According to Merriam Webster, the definition of prayer is a petition to God in word or thought, and earnest request or wish. Psalm 5: 3 (AMP) says, "In the morning, O Lord, You will hear my voice; In the morning I will prepare (a prayer and a sacrifice) for You and watch and wait (for You to speak to my heart)."

Prayer is of vital importance in life because we need the connection with God. The webinar, Fearless Prayer Warrior, helped me learn how to pray effectively. I have purchased many books about prayer. I have learned that I need to be praying warfare prayers instead of mediocre ones because we are at war with the devil. He is not playing with any of us. He is out to kill, steal, and destroy our lives, destiny, or family. Now I don't have to accept when he tries to attack my body, finances, family, or business. I will put the Word on that rascal, and he must flee. He knows that his time is short. He doesn't have any power over us because we sit in heavenly places with Jesus.

We are walking in the same power that raised Jesus from the dead. "Oh, no! Satan, the blood of Jesus is against you. You have no authority or right to attack my family or me." When the blood of Jesus is present on your life, the enemy can't do anything to you. The children of Israel when they put the blood of a lamb on the doorposts, this was a symbolic representation that they were covered from destruction destined for the people at that time. When the death angel came to kill all the first born, all the houses with the blood on the doorposts that belonging to the children of Israel were spared. The first-born children and the cattle belonging to the Egyptians died. Pharaoh then agreed to let the children of Israel go. They didn't leave empty-handed either. They left with the spoils (wealth) of the Egyptians. We, too, are covered by the blood, which averts all danger.

I learned to pray from the Word of God for a matter. We have the power to bind and loose the Word of God. Matthew 16:19 (AMP) says, "I will give you the keys (authority), of the kingdom of heaven; and whatever you bind (forbid, declare to be improper and unlawful) on earth will have (already) been bound in heaven, and whatever you loose (permit, declare lawful) on earth will have (already) been loosed in heaven."

James 5:16 (AMP) says, "Therefore, confess your sins to one another (your false steps, your offenses), and pray for one another, that you may be healed and restored. The heartfelt and persistent prayer of a righteous man(believer) can accomplish much (when put into action and made effective by God—it is dynamic and can have tremendous power)."

Prayer is not just you talking to God, but He is talking back to you. We must calm ourselves and listen for His voice. Prayer is one of the most powerful weapons that we have. We can pray in English with understanding or pray in tongues, which is praying directly to God where only He will understand. When we pray in tongues more, it helps build us up.

Jude 1:20 (AMP) states, "But you, beloved, build yourselves up on (the foundation of) your most holy faith (continually progress, rise like an edifice higher and higher), pray in the Holy Spirit." When we are directed by the Holy Spirit to pray in tongues, we don't know what we are praying for, but our spirit prays directly to God on our behalf about a matter. Remember to always pray. There is no way around it. If you want to keep an intimate relationship with God, it is done through prayer. We can never pray too much. Pray without ceasing; all day, every day in our minds, thoughts, written, and spoken word. Pray, and then pray again.

CHAPTER 19

Married for Purpose

In 2008, I met the man who is now my husband. I believed that he was sent to me by God. I had been praying for a husband. I wanted someone who loved God and was totally sold out to Christ. We met and dated for over a year. We lived in different counties over an hour away from each other. When we first got married it was hard because I had injured my back. I was commuting back and forth from Bacon County to Toombs County to work. The job was very stressful because I had to deal with many difficult family members and residents. I was on my feet almost the whole eight hours because they were always short of nurses. All of this took its toll on my back. So, I ended up quitting the job because the pain was unbearable. I lost all my health insurance because of having to quit the job. I was burned out from the job as well. At that point, I never wanted to work in another nursing home. I would visit but working in one was out of the question. I once loved nursing, but it became overwhelmingly burdensome both physically and emotionally. As a result, we were living off one income.

My husband had his own business years before we met. Now that I look back at all the things that we went through, I know that it was warfare. The enemy didn't want our marriage to last but we have fought through the tough times. Together, we learned how to pray, fast, read the Word, and converse about our lives. Of course, with God as the third strand of the cord, we have been able to stay together and grow together. We have taken classes on online, webinars, bought and read books. Also, we listen to teachings on our specific gifts and want to grow g in the things of God. We must remain teachable in the things of God. I don't ever want to think that I have learned it all, because there is always more to learn.

Bill Johnson states, in "God Hides Things to Be Found," "The Bible indicates that God receives more glory when He conceals, rather than making things obvious. It is more glorious for Him to hide and have us seek. Mysteries are our inheritance.[29] The Word says that God will fill those who hunger and thirst after righteousness for His name sake. Today my husband and I are stronger together because we realize that it is not just about us, but it is about so much more. It is about the lives that God have set for us to touch with His love and grace.

I get up every morning to join a prayer line at 6 am.[30] I started on it in November 2018. I wake up seeking the Lord in the mornings and praying in tongues. It has really helped me grow closer to Christ. I no longer have just weekend visits with Christ, but I now have a genuine relationship with Him. It is so much sweeter than I have ever known. I have a joy now inside that doesn't come from stuff. My joy comes from knowing that God loves me and cares about me. I can truly feel the love of a Father, which I never experienced in the natural. God is my Abba Father. He will always be there for me whenever I need Him. When I have an issue, I will pray and believe that He will take care of everything that I need. I must decree and declare and walk in the authority that He has given me. I continue to pray the Scriptures back to God and reminding Him of His word. Victory is already ours. The devil is a liar and everything that he could ever say is a lie. The truth is not in him anywhere. He is the father of lies, so anything he says is not true.

What God says about me is true. I am who God says I am, and I can do what God says I can do. I don't need anyone to cosign on it because what God says about the matter is what will stand. I stand on the truth and the word of God is the only truth that will stand the test of time. When everything else fails, God's word stands. We must continue to go through deliverance from time to time because if we are living in this world, we will have issues. But our issues don't have to consume us. We are overcomers if we stay rooted and grounded in Christ. We will win every time. There is nothing that we can ever go through that God doesn't have an answer for. When we pray and seek Him for the solution to our problems. He will always help us through the storms in life.

PRAYER

Father God, in the name of Jesus, I pray that You bless everyone who will read this book. Lord, we break every binding spirit that is not like God in our lives. Lord, if anyone hasn't confessed You as being their Lord and savior, give them the chance right now to make You Lord over their life.

Romans 10:9-10 (Amp) says, "Because if you acknowledge and confess with your mouth that Jesus is Lord (recognizing His power, authority, and majesty as God), and believe in your heart that God raised Him from the dead, you will be saved." "For with the heart a person believes (in Christ as Savior) resulting in his justification (that is, being made righteous—being freed of the guilt of sin and made acceptable to God); and with the mouth he acknowledges and confesses (his faith openly), resulting in and confirming (his) salvation."

Lord, I come into agreement with your word. Now I have been saved and set free from sin and death. Lord, remove the people that I have around me that do not come into an agreement with the new life that I have in you. Lord, I ask that you put the right people around me that would help me grow closer to You and Your word. Lord, I thank You for giving me a new lease on life. I don't have to keep going around in circles and getting nothing accomplished. Lord, do a work in me so when people see me, they will see the love of Christ radiating from within me in Jesus' name.

Lord, I pull down every stronghold, soul ties, and any other things that would separate me from You in Jesus' name. Lord, heal every broken place in my life and go deep down in my heart. Remove the heart of stone and give me a heart of flesh that will be sensitive to Your Holy Spirit in Jesus' name. Lord, make all things new in my life so I will go on to be all that You have called me to be in this world. Lord, remind me to always consult you first before I make any kind of decisions in my life, whether it be small or major. Lord, you said in Your word that if we need wisdom we are to ask of God, and You will give it to them. I declare that wisdom will come upon me and rule and reign in their lives right now in Jesus name. Lord, we give You all the glory, honor and praise for what You are getting ready to do in my life right now in Jesus' name. Lord, I pray that I will surrender my will for Your will in Jesus' name. You know what is best for every one of us in Jesus' name. Lord, we thank you in advance for the mountains moving in my life in Jesus' name. Amen.

About The Author

La Rose Angela Richardson is the wife of Richard Richardson and the mother of Satara Cowan. She has one granddaughter, Allara Cowan. She has lived in the Southeast Georgia area for all of her life. La Rose has worked in the nursing field for a total of twenty-two years. First, as a C.N.A. for eight years, then going further in her studies for Practical Nursing. She graduated from Southeastern Technical Institute in June 1997 with a degree in Practical Nursing. She worked at a local nursing home in Vidalia, GA, for 14 years as an L.P.N. In 2009 she married Richard Richardson and moved to the city of Alma, GA, where they resided for nine years.

La Rose and her husband moved to Baxley, GA, in June 2018 where they now live. She is one of the co-authors of "It Cost Me Everything," that was written with Prophetess Kimberly Moses. Presently, LaRose attends Prophetess Kimberly Moses's Prayer line that meets Monday through

Friday at 6 am and 12 pm. She went to Crossland Christian University's Alma campus. Later she graduated with a Master's of Arts Degree in Theology on May 30, 2015, in Orlando, FL. She was ordained on May 29, 2015, at an Ordination service before graduation at Crossland Christian University.

She is a poetry writer with several poems published in "Our great Modern Poets." She continued to pursue her education later graduating with a Doctor's Degree in Theology from Crossland Christian University. She joined the prayer line "Tongues of Fire" in November 2018 with Prophetess Kimberly Moses. She has been greatly empowered by praying in tongues for an hour daily. Every wound or set back that she has gone through in her life has been for a purpose that was far greater than she could ever understand. All the troubles and trials were just a push to her so she could walk into her God-given destiny.

References

1. "Soul." Merriam-Webster.com. 2019. https://www.merriam-webster.com accessed January 2019.
2. Strong's Concordance # 5315 "nephesh" accessed January 2019.
3. Eckhardt, John. God's Covenant With You For Deliverance & Freedom. Accessed January 2019.
4. "Malice." Merriam-Webster.com. 2019. https.//www. Merriam-Webster.com/dictionary accessed January 2019.
5. "Venom." Merriam-Webster.com. 2019. https.//www.Merrian-Webster.com/dictionary accessed January 2019
6. Biblereason.com accessed January 2019 https.//Merriam-Webster.com/dictionary
7. Old Man, Perfectingofthesaints.com accessed January 2019 https.//www.Merriam-Webster.com/dictionary
8. "Bitterness."Merriam-Webster.com. https.//www.Merriam-Webster.com/dictionary accessed January 2019

9. "Bitterness." Greatbiblestudy.com accessed January 2019
10. "Fear." Merriam-Webster.com. https.//www. Merriam-Webster.com/dictionary accessed January 2019
11. "Phobias." https.//www.MedicalNewsToday.com accessed January 2019
12. "Phobias."Merriam-Webster.com. https.//www.Merriam-Webster.com/dictionary accessed January 2019
13. Eckhardt, John. Deliverance, Prayers that Rout Demons. accessed January 2019
14. Eckhardt, John. Fasting For Breakthrough & Deliverance accessed January 2019
15. Fasting at Jentezenfranflin.org accessed January 2019
16. "Self-Doubt."Merriam-Webster.com. https.//www. Merriam-Webster.com/dictionary accessed January 2019
17. Benefits of Praying In Tongues by Kcm.org accessed January 2019
18. "Low Self-Esteem." Merriam-Webster.com. https.//www.Merriam-Webster.com/dictionary accessed January 2019

19. "Rejection." Merriam-Webster.com. https.//www. Merriam-Webster.com/dictionary accessed January 2019
20. "Hopelessness." Merriam-Webster.com. https.//www. Merriam-Webster.com/dictionary accessed January 2019
21. "Self-Hatred." Merriam-Webster.com https.//www. Merriam-Webster.com/dictionary accessed January 2019
22. King, Rebecca L. 40 Day fast accessed January 2019
23. "Insecurities." Merriam-Webster.com. https.//www.Merriam-Webster.com/dictionary accessed January 2019
24. Weidners, Robin. Overcoming Insecurities In A Woman's Life. Accessed January 2019
25. "Depression." Ask-Angels.com accessed January 2019
26. Einstein, Albert. Quote.
27. Fearless Prayer Warriors by Prophetess Valora Cole accessed November through January 2019 10 week webinar.
28. "Prayer." Merriam-Webster.com. https.//www. Merriam-Webster.com/dictionary accessed January 2019

29. Johnson, Bill. God Hides Things To Be Found.
30. Tongues Of Fire by Prophetess Kimberly Moses, accessed November 2018 until present time 6 am and 12 pm Monday through Friday (712)-770-4160 access code 673436#

Index

A

abandonment, 1, 47
abilities, 13, 27–28, 46, 79
altercation, 53
anxiety, 19, 74
arrangements, 49
authority, 21, 86–87, 92–93

B

believer, 5, 10, 28–29, 87
bitterness, 11–12, 19, 44, 98–99
blood pressure, 18, 78

C

cancer, 12, 17
celibate, 58
children, 1, 3, 5, 17–19, 37, 47, 86–87
Christ, 9, 19, 26, 32–33, 35, 37, 43, 49, 58, 82–83, 89, 91, 93
Christians, 8, 17, 19, 21, 26, 28

compromise, 58
covenant, 4, 98
curses, 16, 18

D

death, 39, 44, 67, 78, 94
declarations, 34
deliverance, 2, 4–5, 15, 19, 34, 92, 99
depression, 77–78, 81, 100
devil, 4, 21–23, 30, 75–76, 86, 92
dream, 62–63, 68, 72

E

enemy, 5, 30, 75, 86, 90
expectation, 39

F

fasting, 19, 21, 23–24, 99
father, 2–3, 17, 24, 48–49, 92
fear, 13–15, 19, 74, 99

G

garment, 40–41
generations, 16–18
glory, 24, 29, 83, 91, 95
God, 3–5, 8–9, 15–16, 18, 20–25, 27–35, 37–38, 45–46, 48–49, 58–59, 63, 68–72, 75–76, 82–83, 87–93
grace, 4, 28, 31, 63, 68, 91
grief, 11, 39, 49, 61, 68, 71

H

healing, 3, 5, 9, 11–12, 15, 17, 19, 21, 23–25, 29, 31, 35, 37, 41–42, 49
heart, 1, 4, 8, 11, 28, 31, 57, 85, 93–94
heaven, 66, 68, 87
help, 34, 36, 38, 48, 68, 71, 78–79, 82, 93–94
Holy, 9, 22, 88
hopelessness, 39–40, 44, 77, 100
hospital, 61–68
humiliation, 14

I

improvement, 39
iniquities, 16, 18
intercession, 72

J

jealous, 16

L

Lord, 5, 9, 16, 20, 23, 36–38, 58, 68–69, 71–72, 74, 85, 91, 93–95
lusts, 9–10

M

malice, 7–8, 98
manifest, 22, 78
marriage, 52, 58–59, 90
miracles, 26, 41, 83
molestation, 1, 51
money, 40, 55, 76
mountains, 20, 95

N

nationality, 46

P

pain, 11, 39–40, 66, 79, 90
pastor, 64, 72
peace, 27–29, 70–72, 75
phobias, 13–15, 99
pneumonia, 65
power, 10, 13, 20–21, 23–24, 26, 76, 80, 83, 86–87, 93
praise, 28, 58, 83, 95
prayer, 23–25, 27, 59, 68–69, 72, 76, 85–88, 93, 99–100
praying, 22, 29–30, 68, 72, 88–89, 91, 97, 99
Prophetic, 83

Q

quitting, 53, 90

R

rejection, 2–3, 5, 36, 38, 100
relationship, 2, 5, 34, 50, 57, 59, 76, 91
responsibility, 31, 47
revival, 56, 83
righteousness, 9, 35, 91

S

salvation, 82, 94
security, 76
self-control, 13
self-doubt, 27
shame, 43–44
snakes, 7, 71
souls, 1, 3–5, 7, 9, 15, 57
strength, 68, 70–71, 74, 83
strongholds, 5, 94
surrender, 37, 82, 95

T

thanksgiving, 27
time, 12, 18, 23, 33–34, 47–49, 52, 55–56, 58, 61–62, 67–72, 78, 83, 86, 92–93
tongues, 29–30, 88, 99, 101
trauma, 1–2, 5
trials, 68, 97
trust, 20, 30
truth, 45, 75, 92

U

unconfident, 74

V

venom, 7–8, 98
victory, 25, 92
voice, 85, 88

W

water, 15, 20, 25
weapons, 30, 88
wisdom, 95
worship, 16, 42, 83
wounds, 6, 57, 97

X

X-rays, 61–62

www.ingramcontent.com/pod-product-compliance
Lightning Source LLC
Chambersburg PA
CBHW052156110526
44591CB00012B/1971

9781946756688